AF590845

Printed in the United States of America

First Printing, 2017

ISBN 978-1-378-04289-0

Tarik A Hodge
410 W, Grand Blvd,
Detroit, MI. 48216
www.facebook.com/Thisrockministriescogic/

Methods of Evangelism

By

Tarik A. Hodge Sr.

Two God sent mentors; Lions of Faith.

Pastor Ronald Larry Griffin

May your example of love for the flock, Leadership of men and your enduring dedication to the Cross of Christ live on in the hearts and minds of all who follow Christ.

(The Late) Kenneth Wallace Hodge

The embodiment of perseverance, dedication to the just cause, defender of the weak, voice of assurance, an encouragement to the faithful; you who would not die, may peace be upon you forever.

Table of Contents

Preface

If you have ever heard the saying there is more than one way to skin a cat; you are in good standing.

In other words, with anything there are multiple methods or approaches to accomplish a goal.

In my opinion; evangelism is no different. Just like multiple tools in the drawer; no one is more valuable than the other. The result is that the job gets done.

This little book will summarize three of those methods, exploring the pros and cons of each. As always; the tools don't make the mechanic, however the best mechanic with no tools will find it hard to repair the car.

In other words, these methods are simply tools in for your tool box; The Holy Ghost will assist you in your time of need.

(Matthew 10:19 – Luke 12:12)

Methods
of
Evangelism

Chapter One

Intellectual Methods:

Summary of the Intellectual method

"...Be transformed by the renewing of your minds" The Apostle Paul speaks of the transformation of the mind as essential for two things. One not being conformed to this world and two being in a state of spiritual transformation. These two ideas in this one scripture speaks to the heart of the intellectual method of evangelism. Simply put, it means to speak in an intelligent matter about a subject. In this case the subject is God, more directly the God as manifested in the persona of one we call Jesus. There are some who will attain the knowledge of who Jesus is through reason and intellect. Consider Nicodemus. He did not come to Jesus because he had a relationship with him, this would not have worked. He did not come to Jesus because he had a sick child and needed help. He had prior knowledge that a person would come, he had a clear (birds eye) view of Jesus and how we interacted with others. More importantly he concluded that the only way Jesus could do these things is that God had sent him. Nicodemus knew the facts of what Jesus did. And by those facts conclude that God sent him. Two thousand years later, CS Lewis concluded much the same. "Either Jesus was indeed just who he said he was or he was a lunatic who died for nothing" one thing is for sure when the facts of what Jesus did is pointed out and the fact that only Jesus can save in an intelligent manner only one conclusion can be drawn; acceptance as the son of God or rejection completely! Consider this point: all religions have a system of right and wrong. All religions have a genesis (point of origin). All religions have a basis for existing and a person or persons on a path seeking righteousness. The simple fact is; none of the (non-Christian) religions have a person who was born without the assistance of man, possess any record of having healed, fed, delivered and serve as a sacrifice for all men. Second point to consider: not only does Jesus claim to be the son of God but God in the flesh! At the same time, this same Jesus pays the price for the debt of sin. All debt can be paid with the mere acceptance that he is who he says he is. On these two points alone no one can intelligently reject him. Jesus is the only religion that offers the absolute assurance that your debt is paid. Jesus is the only religion that defines your debt as paid in full and your status in heaven is an open door with reserve seating.

In summary: Intellectual Evangelism is simply speaking to the mind the fact of who Jesus is,

what he has done, why he came and how he is unique to all other paths.

Advantages of using this method— 1. This method allows one to compare Jesus to any other religion and show clear concise reasons why Jesus is (a) the only path to Heaven and true right standing with God. (b) all other paths fall short of heaven's gate and thus fall far beyond the reach of the mercies of God. The Hindu recognizes sin and the price for sin must be paid. Sadly, the Hindu can never know how long it will take to pay for this sin...how many life times will it take to pay for the debt of sin? He can never know. The Muslim recognizes sin and the price for sin must be paid. Sadly, the Muslim will never know for sure if that debt is paid. No matter how many good work; he will never have an assurance. The Christian knows that his debt is paid. This is the very pantheon of the Christian religion we don't practice holiness to become holy, we practice holiness because we are declared holy.

Disadvantages of using this method—This method did not work (even) for Jesus. And certainly, none of the apostles. The whole purpose (besides the total misunderstanding of human biology) the statement that "with the heart man believes" is that the head is the greatest deceiver of the entire body. *"Paul said that the Gospel to the Greek is foolish and the Jew requires great signs' 1 Corinthians 1:20"*. It is intellectually dishonest to say that one believes Jesus to be a prophet God who was born by the spoken will of the Father and then in the same breath deny that son-ship' to the Father caused him to be. It is intellectually dishonest to suggest that being a son of Abraham gives one the right to reject a son of

Abraham sent by God to fulfill the promise of Abraham (made by God) waiting for the Messiah while rejecting the Messiah. It is intellectually dishonest to say that if one commits a sin and he dies he will come back as a roach or mouse get another chance die become and antelope need another chance die become a grizzly bear eat said antelope who dies and becomes a gazelle on an on until finally one day come back live prosperous and die and go to heaven. very intelligent people believe these very ideas over simple argument of the Gospel. The argument of the Gospel is simple. "if someone paid your bar tab, you say thank you" (one would not show up to pay the same bill twice). If someone pays your light bill, you say thank you. Jesus paid your sin bill, just say thank you. This argument is rejected as foolishness by billions of so called intelligent people. In summary: The Argument of Intellectual evangelism is dependent upon people having the capacity to draw a logical conclusion when presented with the facts.

Chapter Two

Relational Method:

The Relational Method of Evangelism is the deliberate continual interaction between saint and sinner for introducing and demonstrating the good news of Christ. One is building a relationship centered on demonstrating the sustaining love of Christ that ultimately leads the sinner to the decision that Christ is the only answer for his life. Dr. Ogden (DE) speaks to the matter this way "intimate, accountable relationships, centered on God's word would result in self-initiating, reproducing disciples of Jesus" ***The advantage*** of this big picture, long view approach is never more amplified than the historical implications we find in scripture. On more than one occasion we find Jesus Preaching the Gospel at a retreat in the middle of nowhere. Over 20,000 people are in attendance, at least 5000 men not counting women and children were fed spiritual, and then physically; yet not one record of one person getting converted at that meeting. Matthew, reports a large contingent followed Jesus and listen to his teaching however when he preached a Sunday morning message that they did not agree with, they all left. Not one was converted. One the other hand one need not go far to recognize this truth. Jesus deliberately, personally over a three-year period took twelve men of various backgrounds, stages and challenges in life. Engaged, interacted built and sustained a relationship centered on God's Word that lead to the conversion that changed the world forever. ***The Disadvantages of this method:*** There is a risk of conformation associated with the sustained interaction of peoples. Paul speaks to this in Romans 12:1-2 “be not conformed to this world...”, Dr. Townsend says it this way, interaction must be "Christ centered and accountable" just having a relationship for relationship has never worked in the history of man. Eve, Lott, Isaiah and many others have proven that if you maintain a relationship with an unsaved group of people and Christ is not at the center of your relationship the saved mind loses its trans-formative guard and thus risk being conformed. As Dr. Ogden intimates the relationship must be "Christ Centered and Accountable" for true relational evangelism to work.

Chapter Three

Confrontational Method:

The Direct, Purpose driven encounters are an effective tool in the arsenal of the evangelistic effort. In the days, long before now (some might call it the "old days") the vacuum cleaner salesman would knock on the door when the lady of the house opened the door he would toss a bag of dirt on her nice cleaned carpet. This positioned the salesman to present a solution to an open, obvious problem that when her own vacuum cleaner failed to remove the stain he had the ultimate solution and the sale was made. This is the nature of confrontational evangelism. Causing a person to see that they have a stain in their life that did not originate from them and cannot be removed by them. In other words; there is no other method by which man can be cleansed accept with the blood of Jesus. Isaiah saw the purity and glory of God in contrast he saw himself and became undone. In the example; the lady did nothing to contribute to her problem. She did not put the stain on the floor and it was apparent that she could do nothing to remove it and time is running out. Confrontational evangelism points out to man that he was born in sin, fashioned in iniquity of original sin and time is running out. No work, no effort, on his part can ever suffice for the condition by which he is judged. Jesus sat on the throne (the cross) judged the whole world guilty of sin, worthy of hell; he then took the penalty of death onto himself, went to hell and rose from the dead leaving sin and death in hell where they belong. No one else ever made this claim. To summarize: confrontational evangelism is the art of pointing out the condition of sin (regardless of the persons actions) allowing the person to conclude that there is no other means of obtaining Salvation than through the Blood of Christ.

The Advantage of this method: This method is the most direct of all the others. It removes any ambiguity with regards to the purpose of the encounter, it demands and answer at "the point of sale" it defies any logical argument while creating a logic based argument. The "I'm a good person" defense is nullified, truthfully (good people go to hell everyday) It obliterates the "many paths to heaven argument" (there is only one) it speaks to directly to the heart of sin – not "the sin, action" but the condition. It destroys the "you deserve to burn in hell argument" frankly we all do. That was the point of Jesus death – he died in our place. The obstacle created by the "you're a sinner" because you committed sin argument is removed from the equation. It portrays the "sinner" as a child born with a terminal illness (sin) the child cannot heal himself...

The Disadvantages to this method: Simplicity often becomes the enemy of its own conclusion. This Pauline approach often creates the same environment that fed Paul's greatest desire "that the Jews might be saved". The form of Godliness is a powerful drug that blinds the practitioner. Many religions place a heavy Garment of piety completely adorned with the robe of suffering for "bad deeds". Sadly, the garment is so heavy, the wearer often lacks the strength to cast it off and come to Christ. The ***second*** and most common disadvantage to this method is *improper application*. History reveals that the word confrontation is often confused with antagonism. Believe it or not, it is possible to approach (confront) a person without insulting (antagonizing) them. The confusion between [confrontation and antagonism] has given the church a very bad reputation; (creating an "us against them" approach) to Christianity that distracts from the purpose of confrontation and arms the enemies of Christ with the argument of "see that is why I am not Christian". The multitude of harmful, Geo-political implications are innumerable in scope whose fragments litter the landscape of global outreach efforts erroneously identified as confrontational evangelism.

Chapter Four—

The ***Application***

The application of These Methods to my own Life: (My testimonies)

Confrontational Evangelism in my life can be summarized by this very personal historical event. (maybe 30 years ago) On the way back from youth a choir convention held at a large Pentecostal Church on the South side of Chicago (around midnight) my car (filled with three additional African American Young Males, including myself) attracted the attention of a patrol car operated by two European Officers; one male and the other female. Prior to this I set my cruise control to the speed limit, 45mph. (so, we were not speeding) we just encountered a powerful out-pouring of the Holy Ghost; we were on our way (guilty of nothing more than the combination of skin color, age and gender) I took comfort in the fact that prior to the trip my Grandmother took me downtown (Detroit) to make sure that my driving record was clean. So, the officers pulled over this dark (newer) car filled with four AAYM from Detroit "surely, they have drugs on the, the officer said, "they all do" check to see if the car is stolen as they illegally searched my car, no drugs existed the short version; [I was arrested for unpaid parking tickets] I thought why is God letting this terrible thing happen to me? What did I do to deserve this? The supervising officer arresting me told the trainee that they expect find something when got to the station. We arrive at the station and the officer locks me in with an individual whose life was in trouble...he was not saved; he had been a car accident. I wasted no time wondering why I was there. No more wondering why God was letting this happen to me. That man needed to hear the

Gospel of Jesus Christ (and my father was on his way too bail me out so I had very little time) I asked had he ever heard of Jesus Christ? He replied, yes but he did not listen...I told him the only reason I was there in that cell with him is that God wanted to speak to him. I preached the Gospel to him from the context of "original" sin, not his actions but the original sin nature that he was born in. if he changed all of his actions if he cleaned up his whole life (without Jesus) he would still be in the same wretched state the officers came and told me that I could not preach on Government property, I reminded them that had I not been arrested I would not be here and since I committed no crime this is the only explanation that exist. for this man's sake was I brought here this night that he may have one more chance to surrender to Christ. They asked him, “is he being bothered?” the man told him “I am twice his size and strength, if I wanted him to shut up, I could, besides; he's right, I need to hear and this time I am listening” as I continued and closed they were pulling me out of the cell “it’s time to go! “Your dad is here” (the officer said) but the music that I heard is the man telling me (as they pulled me away) “I am ready to receive this Jesus you been talking about” “I want him in my heart” I never saw that man again. My Father could not believe that through that ordeal the only thing on my mind was a stranger getting saved. I never had the opportunity to talk to that man again. On many occasion the Spirit has moved me to “properly apply the “confrontation” approach to evangelism.

Sometime later, I was painting a building for a

business owner in a particularly rough neighborhood in the City of Highland Park, Mi., as I was painting this massive building an individual happened to walk by and admired the work; I began to speak with him and immediately turned the conversation toward his relationship with the Lord. I simply began to tell him what the Lord will do for him and he asked me how could I know this, and as I began to tell him what the Lord did for me; how I was once homeless, out of doors on the streets of Chicago; how he saved my soul, how he made it possible for me to exploit my talents for profit, as I told him what he did for me he began to see that this same Jesus loved him as well and could do the same. His bus came and he had to go; we shook hands, hugged and off he went. A few months later; I heard a voice yelling out my name; yelling from down the street; this massive individual runs up to me (I forgot who he was) hugs me and grabs me by both shoulders looks down at me with a smile, saying "Thank you!" you saved my life; he went on to say, "the day I met you outside of that building, I was going to rob you, I was just waiting for the right moment; but you kept talking...you see, I had just gotten out of prison for armed robbery and I needed some money, but you kept telling about the Lord and it messed me up inside. He went on to tell me that "I got saved, I have not robbed anybody since, I started working with this company, my life is turned completely around" Thank you! "if you need anybody jacked, you let me know!" "Thank you, man, thank you for telling me about this Jesus!"

While I have not needed anybody "jacked" I get the sentiment. I never knew his name; his condition, or his life, what I knew is that Jesus had saved my life and could do the same for him. In my experience, evangelism is the planting of the seed; writing upon the table of the hearts of men. Each table is different.

There is no "one size fits all approach"; without the direct guidance of the Holy Ghost (Spirit) none will work. Have confidence when the encounter happens trust that the Holy Spirit of God will give you the right words, the right word and the applicable approach to the condition. There is no limit to the effects of proper evangelism. One can never know the extent to which the simplest effort can have the greatest impact. One can never know how long the person has contemplated the question of Christ and the Cross. Years ago, as a young man I was at a night club and I looked over across the room and saw this stunningly beautiful young lady sitting all alone; I established eye contact, approached her, introduced myself, complimented her smile and asked why she was all alone and not on the dance floor; she responded, "no one asked me to dance" I stretched out my hand and invited her to dance and she took my hand and we walked to the dance floor. We had a wonderful time! One might wonder why was she all alone; she was six feet without heals, (she wore heals) though she was very beautiful, (I am 5'4 with shoes) apparently her height intimidated most of the men; they looked from a safe distance; like little boys the they made jokes of what they would do, but no one had the courage to simply ask the lady to dance. No method of evangelism will ever work if we don't at the very least make the effort; the tree will not grow until it is planted.

It is my sincere hope that this book will encourage you to leave the side-lines, part from your secure section of the room and go be an evangelist for Christ, after all there is a Muslim, a Jew, a Buddhist, a none of the above waiting at the table of life for a sincere, courageous believer to approach, introduce, show some kindness and with an outstretched hand invite them to know who Jesus is.

Someone reached out to me: I was born and raised in the Nation of Islam as Muslim. I prayed five times each day, though it was not required I fasted with my father in observance of Ramadan. My mother taught us to read by three years of age, so by than I read my Qur'an at 5:00 am every morning, (accept Saturdays, cartoons) I attended a Muslim school, and learn to speak Arabic, as time went on I began asking questions; a lot of them, mostly surrounding the idea that one Jesus is in the Qur'an (why) and two where do people go to get born again? "how does one become born again"? If babies come out of the belly than how does a grown person get back in? Supposed the mother is in heaven does that stop one from becoming born again? All these questions and few answers to suffice. One day the sweet old lady from next door asked my father if she could take the boys to church with her; my father (not wanting to hurt her feelings agreed) and off we went; Clark Road Missionary Baptist Church; three Muslim boys, the oldest (me) at age thirteen sitting amid a room full of Christians shouting and praising the Lord. We were like fish out of water. As the music died down and it was time to hear the message the Reverend Evans got up and asked the question "How can a man be born again?" The sermon was from John 3:27, Nicodemus came to Jesus by night asking the very question that I had been asking since I was eight years old. Finally, someone can explain this mystery (I thought to myself) so, I listened and as he preached it became clear; that Jesus was not interested in how long you prayed, how many times, or in what style, he was interested in where your heart was when you prayed. "For with the heart man believes..." (Romans) there is a hadith a (saying) that when a man is on a journey though he traveled that journey of forty days when and if he is confronted with the truth that he is on the wrong path; he must without hesitation bear witness to the truth and seek the right path (even if that means going in a direction opposite to your understanding). I realized at that moment as he preached that the way to reconciliation with God was not limited to prayer and a Pius life but to the acceptance of the gift of Christ. This acceptance was wrought with the obligation of confession that we are born in sin and only through the blood of Christ can we be saved. Confronted with this truth was convicted that the rebirth was a spiritual rebirth, not a physical as I once understood. When the alter call was made; So, I along with my two younger brothers made our way to the alter and gave our lives to the Lord. My father did not take lightly the idea that his three sons left the house that morning as good Muslim children and returned that afternoon as professed Christians. Twenty-Six years later my Father, Mother, Uncles, Aunts and cousins (all who were Muslim came to the knowledge of and confessed Christ as their Lord and Savior.

Chapter 5

Purpose of Evangelism

The purpose of evangelism is not to treat sin as a “crime perpetrated by the practitioner” to wit one seeks to annihilate or prosecute the offending opponent; rather the purpose of evangelism is likened on to a man walking by the river when he hears a cry for help. The normal reaction to a drowning individual is not ridicule the potential victim for being in the situation in the first place; usually one would simply leap into the water, throw a rope out or grab a stick or something for the person to grab onto and be pulled to safety. The point is that, the method to which one seeks to save is not so material to the drowning person. What is important is to the drowning person is that the drowning person knows that you are there to perform the rescue, you are there because you heard the cry for help, you are there filled with compassion to save a living human being from drowning.

We can look at each of the three methods outlined in this book and review with some similarity to methods used in the above analogy; (Intellectually, Confrontational, Relational) v Leap in, throw a rope, grab a long stick. These are but tools deployed to achieve the same outcome; depending on the user, all can be quite helpful. However, each of these can also do much more harm than good, if used improperly. For example; If the user is so only there to show how smart he or she is and make other people fill dumb than the "intellectual method" will more than likely fail. Imagine for a moment if one sees a drowning person and decides to use a stick to reach in and save the person; that would be a great idea. The person can obviously see that the stick is strong and long enough to reach in and pull the victim out of the water.

This is a logical, thoughtful way to help

save a life. Now picture the same scenario played out a little differently, what if when the victim reaches for the stick the person holding the other end raised the stick out of reach of the victim. The trust gained by the person holding the stick has now been lost. The hope presented is now gone and both participants are condemned to the reality of this most cruel outcome.

Imagine the person seeking to save decides to leap into the water and save the drowning person, great idea, only if one can swim; if not, then both will soon need assistance and the outcome is now worse than ever. Suppose there is a rope handy, terrific; unless the rope (your relationship to God) is frail and the both are pulled; the outcome is worse.

Chapter 6

The Safe Zone:

We are not here to show how smart we are, how saved we are or how much real-estate we will have in heaven; we are here to save a life! The person to whom we are rendering this service must be made aware from the outset that they are in a "judge free zone" this safe zone allows the conviction, repentance and confession process to work. Regardless of the method one deploys if the environment is not perceived as being safe, if the victim feels judged, ashamed or condemned, the outcome can be much worse than the former state.

Saving the life of the victim and

maintaining our relationship with Christ must be at the center of evangelism. Love must be the foundation with which we stand. Beating someone over the head with a stick, binding them with the rope of condemnation, joining them in the sin can impede the progress of evangelism and in fact leave the victim and the even the rescuer in a state worse than before.

Paul's argument to the Corinthian Church (1 Corinthians 13:2) was principally, that all the tools that God provides all of the efforts that deploy to advance the kingdom of God and the salvation of his people must be built on the foundation of Love. Love for the God, and Love for the people. If this in fact is the foundation of one's purpose than don't worry; God will provide plenty of opportunity for the ministry of evangelism to grow and prosper. The life experiences that one has lived both in and out of the Gospel serves as preparation for the evangelist.

Chapter 7

The Perception of Evangelism

In the defense to all who make the effort and perhaps reap unintended results or less than positive outcomes. Perhaps this chapter may be of some comfort. In my opinion, the Church overall has put forth or fed perhaps a perception that has permeated itself throughout the ministry of outreach. For example, consider the term Saint and Sinner...the perception that one draws are a somewhat adversarial relationship between the evangelist' and the evangelized'. With this scenario, one can see how the idea of prosecutor line of questioning worked its way into the realm of evangelism. The representatives often will approach a person as though the pursuing the case of saint v sinner to wit the prosecution makes the case that the sinner is such an awful person that they should be found guilty by the jury (of their peers) and sent off to the “bottomless pit” in the center of the earth, that happens to be on fire, that by the way is filled with gnashing of teeth, which somehow there are rich people down there asking for water to be put on his tong and the fire burns forever...and of course why not throw some alligators in there to make it more scary of course can be avoided if they simply admit guilt and throw themselves onto the mercy of the court then hallelujah Jesus can show them mercy. While this pitch may work with the kids and maybe some adults, history reveals that this approach has a “short shelf life”.

Galatians 6:1 KJV presents a more workable perception that one should foster. 6 ***Brethren***, if a man be ***overtaken*** in a fault, ye which are spiritual, ***restore*** such a one in the spirit of meekness; ***considering thyself***, lest thou also be tempted.

2 ***Bear ye*** one another's burdens, and so fulfill the law of Christ.

Notice the key words with one can readily draw the conclusion that evangelism is anything but adversarial. There is no "us v them" we are brothers and sisters made in the image of God. Like different pieces of beautiful furniture made by the same manufacture resting in different homes and used for very different purposes some overtime as been exposed to experiences that leaves indelible marks for all the world to see. The Bible calls them **"faults"**. Notice the writer refers to the effort with the word "restore". To restore something is not simply returning to its former glory, but to make it stronger than it was before. Look at the word, "overtaken" this implies a struggle has taken place. Imagine for a moment walking down the street and you hear screaming "help, help please help, I'm being robbed please help me!!!! what is the proper response? a. tell the women her screaming is improper, not very lady like and if she simply read this pamphlet and ask Jesus to forgive her she will be okay (meanwhile the robber is still trying to snatch her purse) b. join in with the robber and take her purse because after all she should not have been in that neighborhood at that time of night? Or C. join in with the woman as she is sister being robbed and defend her against the robber? To any reasonable person, I would imagine c. to be the obvious choice of the three. The Biblical principal pointed out in Galatians is that regardless of how the person that we are attempting to evangelize, got to this place; they are not the enemy! They are a part of the family. When a member of the family is attacked the whole family is attacked. Paul argues that this intervention must be made with a spirit or attitude befitting an instrument of God. Meekness, humility, grace is far more powerful a tool than the amount of scriptures one has memorized. Notice that this attitude or "spirit" comes with a warning; not to the target of the rescue but to the rescuer. We are required by law to see in ourselves the person that does not look like us; and yet is exactly like us, wrought with human frailties, weakness, desires, fears and temptations. The imperative nature that the apostle Paul demands of the Church at Galatia and by extension the Church at Large rest on the eleventh commandment meted out by Jesus himself..." Love your neighbor as you love yourself" all the "thou shalt not's" that we have memorized in the Old Testament rest on this one principal. One cannot even Love God, much less his creation unless one's self is first loved. Paul warns that we too can find ourselves in the very same boat; therefore, we have no room to condemn the brother or sister "taken" that's not our mission. As an evangelist, we are on a global ***rescue*** mission both in the Church and out.

BIBLIOGRAPHY—

References

Gutierrez, B., (2011). Living Out the Mind of Christ., Virginia Beach, VA., Academy Publishing

Page 20

Early, D., & Wheeler, D. (2010). *Evangelism Is...* Nashville, TN., Academy Publishing Group.

Page 79

Ogden, G., (1998). Discipleship Essentials., Downers Grove, ILL., Intervarsity Press,

Page 9

About the Author:

Tarik A. Hodge is currently the Pastor and Founder of This Rock Ministries Church of God in Christ in Detroit, Michigan.

Pastor Hodge is a Graduate of the National School of Theology.

Pastor Hodge is a current Student of Liberty Baptist Theological Seminary.

Pastor Hodge is married to his lovely wife Keisha T. Hodge together they have three beautiful children.

Pastor Hodge is the Author of two additional books: The Free Christian © 2010 and The Great Commission © 2017

Note:

This book was written in part as an assignment while attending Liberty Baptist Theological Seminary. Evangelism 101

Ms. Bethany L. Emery '03, *Adjunct Professor*

www.ingramcontent.com/pod-product-compliance
Ingram Content Group UK Ltd.
Pitfield, Milton Keynes, MK11 3LW, UK
UKHW020217250726
13967UKWH00001B/43

9 781387 042890